Kids in the Kitchen™
The Library of Multicultural Cooking

FOOD AND RECIPES OF JAPAN

by Theresa M. Beatty

The Rosen Publishing Group's
PowerKids Press™
New York

The recipes in this book are intended for a child to make together with an adult.
Many thanks to Ruth Rosen and her test kitchen.

Published in 1999 by The Rosen Publishing Group, Inc.
29 East 21st Street, New York, NY 10010

First Edition

Book Design: Resa Listort

Photo Credits and Photo Illustrations: Cover photo by John Bentham; p. 7 © Richard Embery/FPG International; pp. 8, 10, 18 by John Novajosky; pp. 9, 19 by Pablo Maldonado; p. 11 by Christine Innamorato; p. 12 © David Bartruff/FPG International; p. 13 © 1995 PhotoDisc Inc.; p. 15 © R. Tesa/International Stock; p. 16 © D. Klesenski/International Stock; p. 20 © Stock Food America/Eising.

Beatty, Theresa M.
    Food and recipes of Japan / by Theresa M. Beatty.
        p.   cm. — (Kids in the kitchen : multicultural cooking)
    Includes index.
    Summary: Describes some of the foods enjoyed in Japan and provides recipes for several popular Japanese dishes.
    ISBN 0-8239-5319-X
    1. Cookery, Japanese—Juvenile literature. 2. Food habits—Japan—Juvenile literature. [1. Food habits—Japan. 2. Cookery, Japanese.] I. Title.
II. Series: Beatty, Theresa M. Kids in the kitchen.
    TX724.5.J3B43 1998
    641.5952—dc21
                                          97-11213
                                              CIP
                                               AC

Manufactured in the United States of America

CONTENTS

Abbreviations

cup = c.   Farenheit = F.   pound = lb.   tablespoon = tbsp.   teaspoon = tsp.

Celsius = C.   kilogram = kilo   liter = l   milliliter = ml

JAPAN

The island country of Japan rests in the Pacific Ocean, just off the coast of the great **continent** (KON-tih-nent) of Asia. Japan is made up of four main islands. They are Hokkaido, Honshu, Kyushu, and Shikoku. There are many smaller islands too, including Okinawa.

The Japanese believe in living in **harmony** (HAR-muh-nee) with nature and respecting its beauty. So they like to enjoy food the way it is found in nature. They use the natural colors and **textures** (TEKS-churz) of foods to create beautiful, tasty meals.

◀ *More than 125 million people live in Japan.*

A FEAST FOR THE EYES

The Japanese believe that the way food looks is just as important as the way it tastes. Green snow peas might be placed next to pink shrimp to make a colorful dish. A Japanese meal is a work of art as much as it is a meal!

Mealtime is also a chance to show off the beautiful dishes or baskets in which food is served. A long dish may have only two or three small items of food on it. This way the beauty of the dish itself can be enjoyed as much as the flavor of the food.

Many Japanese dishes are made to fit in your hand. An important part of Japanese **etiquette** (EH-tih-kit) is lifting your dish close to your chest when eating rice or soup.

Because many Japanese dishes are served with rice, ▶
it's easier to eat from bowls than off of flat plates.

FOODS IN JAPAN

Japanese food has been influenced by many other **cultures** (KUL-cherz) through trade. Bean curd and the use of chopsticks came from China. Potatoes, sweet potatoes, and corn were brought over from Holland about 400 years ago.

Because Japan is surrounded by the ocean, seafood is a big part of Japanese **cuisine** (kwih-ZEEN). But the most important food in Japan is rice. This is because rice grows easily in most parts of Japan. Rice is eaten with almost every meal. Many Japanese soups are made from **dashi** (DAH-shee). This **stock** (STOK) is made from flakes of dried bonito fish and a seaweed called kelp. Seaweed and a large white radish called **daikon** (DY-kohng) are also used in many Japanese recipes.

Suimono Egg and Pea Soup

You will need:

18 peas in pod

6 c. *(1.5 l)* dashi or canned chicken broth

2 tsp. *(10 ml)* soy sauce

6 eggs

HOW TO DO IT:

- Remove peas from pods.
- Simmer dashi or broth in a large pot over medium heat.
- Stir in soy sauce.
- Add peas to pot and simmer for a few moments until peas are tender.
- Remove peas from soup while still bright green and set aside.
- When soup is hot, break eggs gently into pot. Do not mix.
- Allow eggs to cook thoroughly in the soup .
- Next, get six soup bowls ready and place three peas in each bowl.
- Gently remove eggs from soup with slotted spoon and place one egg in each bowl.
- Carefully pour hot soup over egg and peas.

Serves 6

Always ask a grown-up to help you when using knives!
Always ask a grown-up to help you when using the stove or oven!

EATING

Japanese food is prepared in bite-sized pieces. **Portions** (POR-shunz) are small, but many different foods are usually served.

The Japanese use chopsticks to eat instead of knives and forks. Chopsticks are thin sticks made from a strong plant called bamboo. They are held in one hand and used to pick food up from a bowl or plate. Learning to use chopsticks takes some practice. But it is easy to eat Japanese food with them since the food comes in small, ready-to-eat pieces.

Each person in a Japanese home has his or her very own set of chopsticks.

Oyako-Domburi
(Chicken, Mushrooms, and Egg on Rice)

You will need:

- 6 tbsp. *(90 ml)* lemon juice
- 6 tbsp. *(90 ml)* soy sauce
- 1 c. *(250 ml)* dashi or chicken broth
- ½ c. *(125 ml)* uncooked chicken, sliced into bite-sized pieces
- ½ lb. *(.227 kilo)* mushrooms, cleaned and sliced
- 3 onions, peeled, halved, and sliced thin
- 1 carrot, sliced thin, lengthwise
- 1 celery stalk, sliced thin
- 6 eggs
- 1 scallion, sliced thin
- 6 c. *(1.5 l)* cooked rice, steamed or boiled

HOW TO DO IT:

- ❋ In a pot, simmer lemon juice over medium heat.
- ❋ Stir in soy sauce and chicken broth.
- ❋ When broth mixture is hot, add chicken, mushrooms, onions, carrots, and celery. Simmer for 10 to 15 minutes.
- ❋ When well cooked, remove from heat and divide into 6 portions.
- ❋ Place one portion at a time in a frying pan over medium heat.
- ❋ Add a lightly beaten egg and some scallions to each serving.
- ❋ When egg is almost cooked, remove from heat. Place on a plate with 1 cup *(250 ml)* of hot rice. Cover with another plate.
- ❋ Repeat for remaining 5 portions.
- ❋ Remove covers and serve hot.

Serves 6

Always ask a grown-up to help you when using knives!
Always ask a grown-up to help you when using the stove or oven!

FOODS BY THE SEASON

Because nature is important to the Japanese, their food changes with the seasons. This allows people to enjoy the freshest foods. Eggplants are eaten in the summer and special matsutake mushrooms are eaten in the fall. The Japanese look forward to eating the first bonito fish every spring.

Food isn't the only thing that changes with the seasons. The Japanese change their dishes too. For example, glass bowls and dishes are used only in the summer. This is also part of the Japanese **tradition** (truh-DIH-shun) of serving food in a way that pleases both the stomach and the eyes.

Most Japanese dishes look as delicious as they taste.

DIFFERENT PLACES, DIFFERENT FOODS

Because Japan is made up of several islands, the country has a wide range of **climates** (KLY-mits). The northern island of Hokkaido is cold, while the southern islands of Okinawa are warm. Certain foods grow in each of these different places. This is how the many ways of cooking are created.

In Hokkaido, it is too cold to grow rice. There people grow corn and potatoes instead. Dishes called seafood *o-nabe* (oh-NAH-beh) are popular in Hokkaido. These stews can be made with salmon, crab, and scallops.

Instead of rice fields, potato farms are found in places in Japan where the weather is cool. ▶

SUSHI

When Westerners think of Japanese food, one of the first things they think of is **sushi** (SOO-shee). Sushi is a Japanese rice dish. The rice is flavored lightly with vinegar and sometimes salt and sugar.

To make one kind of sushi, cool, cooked rice is rolled together with different kinds of raw seafood, such as tuna, salmon, octopus, squid, or shrimp, in a seaweed wrapper. Some people also put vegetables and eggs in their sushi.

Sushi comes in many forms. It can be rolled into a ball, shaped like a block, or wrapped in seaweed or bamboo leaves.

Preparing all the different types of sushi isn't easy. Most restaurants have sushi chefs, who have been specially trained in the art of making sushi.

17

SUKIYAKI

One of the most popular dishes in Japan is **sukiyaki** (skee-YAH-kee). This meat and vegetable dish is popular with Westerners. What's fun about sukiyaki is that it is usually cooked right at the table!

A chef places a gas burner on the table. He then cooks all the delicious ingredients, including beef, onions, mushrooms, and bean curd. This is all done right in front of the guests!

Beef was **banned** (BAND) in Japan for hundreds of years because of religious reasons. But about 100 years ago, the emperor ruled that the Japanese could eat beef again.

18

Beef Sukiyaki

You will need:

½ c. *(125 ml)* soy sauce

¼ c. *(50 ml)* sugar

½ c. *(125 ml)* dashi or beef broth

2 tbsp. *(30 ml)* vegetable oil

2 lbs. *(.90 kilo)* beef tenderloin, sliced into thin strips

10 scallions, cut into 2-inch *(3 cm)* pieces (green and white parts)

4 stalks celery, sliced on an angle, in ½-inch *(1 1/2 cm)* pieces

12 mushroom caps, sliced

8 oz. *(.22 kilo)* tofu or bean curd, cut into bite-sized cubes

1 8-½ oz. *(.24 kilo)* can bamboo shoots, drained

4 c. *(1 l)* cooked rice

HOW TO DO IT:

❋ Mix soy sauce, sugar, and dashi or broth in a bowl and set aside.

❋ Arrange beef and vegetables on a large platter.

❋ Heat an electric skillet or frying pan to 300 degrees F. *(150 degrees C.)*.

❋ Add oil and heat.

❋ Add the meat. Brown for 2 minutes.

❋ Add the vegetables and the tofu, placing each on its own part of the skillet.

❋ Add the sauce and cook mixture for 6 or 7 minutes, turning gently to prevent burning and keeping all ingredients separate from each other.

❋ Serve at once over rice.

Serves 4–6

Always ask a grown-up to help you when using knives!
Always ask a grown-up to help you when using the stove or oven!

NEW YEAR, SPECIAL FOOD

The most important time of the year in Japan is **Shogatsu** (SHOH-gut-soo), which is a **celebration** (SEL-uh-BRAY-shun) of the New Year. Shops close and people spend a lot of time with their families and friends.

The traditional food for the New Year celebration is *osechi* (oh-SEH-chee). This food is kept in a special box called a *jubako* (JOO-bah-koh). The box is made of many different boxes stacked on top of each other, usually with two to five layers. Each is packed with different kinds of tasty food, such as *tazukuri*, or glazed sardines, *takenoko*, or bamboo shoots, and *kuri kinton*, or chestnuts in a sweet potato paste.

Most Japanese people spend many days preparing the wonderful foods that are served in the New Year boxes.

◀ *Before the New Year,* osechi *sets are sold at department stores for families too busy to cook.*

JAPANESE FOOD OUTSIDE JAPAN

The people who came to the United States and Europe from Japan brought their cooking styles with them. Sushi shops have become very popular in big cities all over the world. But certain ingredients for Japanese cooking are not always available in every part of the world. That's why Japanese food is a bit different outside Japan.

In the United States, people have their own style of preparing Japanese food. You may have heard of a type of sushi called a California roll. This crab and avocado roll is based on traditional sushi but isn't a true Japanese dish. This is because avocado trees are found mainly in America.

Using the recipes in this book, you can share some of the flavors of Japan with your friends and family.

GLOSSARY

banned (BAND) Something that is not allowed.

celebration (SEL-uh-BRAY-shun) A gathering that honors someone or something special.

climate (KLY-mit) The weather conditions of a certain place.

continent (KON-tih-nent) A very large area of land.

cuisine (kwih-ZEEN) A style of cooking.

culture (KUL-cher) The beliefs, customs, art, and religions of a certain group of people.

daikon (DY-kohng) A large white radish.

dashi (DAH-shee) A soup stock that is made from kelp and dried fish flakes.

etiquette (EH-tih-kit) The polite and proper way of doing something.

harmony (HAR-muh-nee) When certain things are in agreement with each other in a pleasing way.

jubako (JOO-bah-koh) A special layered box that holds traditional Japanese New Year food.

o-nabe (oh-NAH-beh) A one-pot stew.

osechi (oh-SEH-chee) Traditional New Year's food that is kept in a *jubako*.

portion (POR-shun) An amount of food served to a person at one time.

Shogatsu (SHOH-gut-soo) The Japanese New Year celebration, which is one of the most important holidays in Japan.

stock (STOK) A liquid in which meat, seafood, or vegetables have been cooked that is used to flavor other recipes.

sukiyaki (skee-YAH-kee) A Japanese dish made with meat and vegetables that is usually cooked right at the table.

sushi (SOO-shee) A famous Japanese rice dish made with seafood and vegetables.

texture (TEKS-chur) How something feels when you touch it.

tradition (truh-DIH-shun) A way of doing something that is passed down through a culture.

INDEX